KEVINWHITAKER

Chicago, Illinois

220 Publishing

(A Division of 220 Communications)

2 Hard 2 Break

Published by 220 Publishing

February 2015

(A Division of 220 Communications)

PO Box 8186

Chicago, IL 60680-8186

www.220communications.com

www.twitter.com/220comm

Cover Design by: LaDale L. Whaley

Interior layout by: Tanesha Lambert, 220 Publishing

ISBN: 978-1-63452-3882

Printed in USA

A RAW STORY ABOUT LIFE FROM
THE STREETS TO THE PULPIT.

Table of Contents

FOREWORD

Apostle Kevin Whitaker and I met when we were teenagers. I have had a unique front row view as a witness to his transformation. Through a more than 3 decade friendship I've seen many iterations of the man who now provides hope and inspiration to thousands, and soon to millions.

When I left Memphis in the mid 1990's I wasn't sure what direction KW (that's what we called him back in the day) was headed. Like so many people we knew before, I imagined that the next time I might see him, would likely be at his own funeral. Given the life he had embraced, that was a real possibility. Danger was always real where we grew up. KW faced Danger head-on, almost challenging it to come after him. I see now how some tough choices forged a monumental and life-saving shift in him.

"2 Hard 2 Break" is more than just a title to a book for me. It was one of the first songs we co-wrote and recorded. Now 20 years later, resurrecting that title for a journey about life's choices proves to me that when you are destined to reach a certain plateau, there is no one or nothing that can hold you back. That is what I believe best describes Apostle Kevin Whitaker. The sub-context for "2 Hard 2 Break" could easily be called "Your Destiny Cannot Be Denied." This is a story about how one man overcame everything life threw at him because he was divinely destined to be greater.

By reading Apostle Whitaker's story, some will see a bit of themselves and the life they are living currently. This isn't a book to draw anyone into the ministry (if you had told me then what KW would become, I would have laughed at you and probably accused you of doing heavy drugs). From the streets, to deacon, to minister, to Apostle, to whatever is next. KW's story is not finished. He is still living and writing what has already been an amazing life.

The challenge for readers of this book is to not look at just the "glory" but to take a serious look at the story, the journey, the highs, the lows and know that no victory comes without a challenge. Know that some of what you find intertwined within yourself is really the product of the life you choose. Sometimes choices are simple. Sometimes, as the rap lyric warns "the hood can take you under." Sometimes, the "hood" tries but in cases like Apostle Whitaker- destiny will not be denied.

"2 Hard 2 Break" is a story has been 40 years in the making. Read it. Enjoy it. Learn from it. Suggest it to friends. But most importantly, reflect upon it: Look back at your life. Look at your current situation. Determine what is trying to break you? It's not where you start that matters. It's how you finish the race called life. Like Apostle Whitaker, you can have a "2 Hard 2 Break" mentality, an unstoppable mindset and an unending desire to reach your destiny.

Glenn Murray
Founder
220 Publishing

2Hard 2Break

INTRODUCTION

There are many things that shape and form the life of an individual. It is those things that are compiled together to make for a rough genesis in life however, if channeled properly; those things will also create within that individual. You see, I was always on a path to becoming what I didn't necessarily know, but I did take a few guesses because I always knew there was something better out there. I guess it's safe to say I was a dreamer and even when my dreams were infiltrated with nightmares, I still dared to dream. Now dreaming alone is not enough, but you gotta do something because the graveyard is filled with the aroma of sweet dreams that have died with someone because they never found a way to break free. They never found a way to manifest what was on the inside or somehow they became overwhelmed with the circumstances of life. They decided dreams don't come true and succumbed to the trap of generational stagnation, which is a family who never produces anyone that ever broke out to do more than the average. It's that always about to do something or always making plans to do something attitude and never actually getting the ball rolling mentality that keeps them stuck. If you never overcome that generational mindset you will always have great limitations that you will never break. I believe that in order for you to break free of those mindsets, you must exemplify a certain passion about life and goals, and a certain enthusiasm about destiny. Like I said, I was always on a path to becoming the person I was destined to be.

I always approached life as if I had somewhere to be and somewhere to go. I can't stress enough how important it is to have that motivation for something or to become someone better. Please note, I am a Pastor now however I won't tell my whole story from a pastor's point of view. I want to keep it as real and raw as I can; however, names have been changed. This is my story, a true story of overcoming. This is a story of resilience and a story of being TOO HARD TO BREAK.

THE GENESIS

(THE BEGINNING)

*Late one night while it's raining and thundering
I'm chilling by myself and thinking to God just
wondering. Please oh Lord can you help me
Tired of these real crooked cops trying to get me.*

Lyrics from the song "Ghetto Heat"

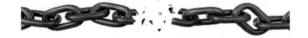

It was the worst of times, as far back as I can remember life was tough. Starting on the south side of Chicago, where it was nothing to see people get robbed on the L-train or to see someone get mugged in the alley. They would even, at times, have to shut my school down because of an escaped prisoner coming through the school snatching children. There were fights every day before, after, and during school. Students would jump teachers and gangs would come to the school to recruit so they could become even more intimidating and all of this was while I was in the 2nd and 3rd grade. I guess you can say that my neighborhood was tough, however no tougher than any other urban neighborhood and while some are fortunate to never see the true workings of the influence of inner city living, there were those of us who were intrigued & those who were afraid and often both groups felt it to be a calling or considered it destiny to get involved.

My first personal encounter with violence was when the neighborhood bully made me sit at the steps and watch his little sister while he rode his bike and went to play with the other kids. He was a few years older and much taller in statue so I must admit I was afraid and then there was this one day that opened me up to a feeling that I would never forget. One day I ran up the stairs and sat down in the living room and my mother asked what was wrong and I replied nothing. She knew that something was bothering me so then she continued to press me for the truth. I finally admitted that the bully had threatened me because I said I would no longer watch his sister and my mother said "The next time he threatens you take a bat and whip his!!!%#@**!!!! up and down this street". So I went back down stairs and about 15 min later he showed up and threatened me and I told him not to. He then said why and I politely went up stairs and got a small miniature bat that had been given to me as a gift. I walked pass my mother who obviously forgot what she had said and I went down stairs and after striking him in the head with the first blow I then proceeded to whip him up and down the street. I will never forget the sense of power and authority that I felt on that day and I believe that day was the foundation of the rest of my life. What I mean is that on the negative side, it showed me the power of violence and on the positive side it set a foundation to overcome my fears. Before this, I was only throwing rocks through windows, having sling shot fights in the alley, which would often turn very bloody. I was stealing candy from the store, which was all bad, but swinging that bat was another kind of feeling that I had so longed for. Then we moved down south and I was thinking we are in the country and I had never seen so many white people in one place at one time, at least as far as I can remember. There wasn't many at my school anyway, so it was kind of shocking. At this time, we are living across Marion Lake Road (Martha's bridge) a place deep in rural area Arkansas where people who didn't have much more than dreams and this was the country for real. It was Fogleman's farm and my grandfather drove tractors and the people down the road still had an outside toilet. My grandparents grew vegetables and had pigs in the back. When it rained, the walk to the bus stop was a long muddy one, but the children who had to walk were good. At least that's what we thought. I started going to school and my first fight was with a white guy, which I under estimated his strength and got the crap beat out of myself. I thought that because I was from Chicago they would automatically bow down to me. I mean I had seen it all and had the attitude that I had done it all and at this point I was only in the forth grade. All of us must understand that growing up in the hood has a way of making us think we are wiser, stronger, and more street savvy than others. I soon found out that these country boys were just as rough. So that created a problem because I'm in an unfamiliar territory and I'm a little shaken because I have to stand alone. I got into many fights but nothing too serious, just little playground battles that many kids have growing up in the hood. At this time I was introduced to church and God. Church was cool because it gave my cousins and me somewhere to go and even though we went to church I truthfully didn't see how we would benefit from it in the now! Just in the bye and bye, but I will admit I was always amazed at the preacher. The Reverend H. W. Showers was his name the pastor of the Rising Sun Missionary Baptist Church and how he would go on and on and on without anyone telling him what to say. Again we are living in the country or rural area of Marion and then we moved to Sunset Arkansas, which is also in Marion but it's a separate little town saturated with a "poverty is ok mentality". We were stagnate and behind the times in every way possible. It was a way of life and it was filled with good times and everyone was for the most part smiling and happy. We didn't have the finest of material things and many lacked the luxury of the basic fundamentals like a car or a floor without holes, at least at my house. It reeked because we burned much of our garbage. Sunset, a place I love, is a typical rural area that you would've seen in many places in the south.

Neighborhood was filled with shotgun houses and shacks, across Marion Lake Road in many instances people still lived on plantations, but sunset was cool. Kids could walk all over the town and play from house to house, or yard to yard unlike Chicago where you had to be careful when you left the street you lived on. Sunset provided a much more liberal and safe atmosphere. I mean everyone at school pretty much dressed on the same level, with the exception of a few, but not enough to affect me. I was cool, didn't at all feel inferior. Life was good and there was a little fighting here and there but we were kids right and kids fight right. Let's not make a big deal out of anything, not knowing that those same kids would grow up to become full fledge criminals and would alter there lives in the worst kind of way.

Fast forward, 1981 my family and I have now moved to West Memphis ark and we are in a much better home, but it's still below average and I'm in the 6th grade. Life then becomes a little more difficult because these kids have better clothes and many of the families have a car or two and now I'm a little intimidated because I can't keep up with the trends. I love my parents, but I wished they would have helped a brother out. My mother, now deceased, and father were average people with ok jobs and perhaps less than perfect budgeting skills and besides that they partied! Nothing is wrong with that but that's what they did and my dad was a strong drug user, mostly marijuana, which was a far stretch from his earlier days of shooting up, which reminds me of why we would have a car and then all of sudden have no car. My cousin, who was as devious as they come, lived down the street and he and I got acquainted. He was an absolutely troubled guy. I didn't really know his father too well and didn't see his mother often. She was a rolling stone and ran with pimps and gangstas back in Chi-town. He was left with his grandparents. I was intrigued by his life because he dressed good and had the girls and although he couldn't really fight, he had a mouth that would make you think that he would attack a bear and rip it to shreds. So I began to hang with him as much as I could. It got me a little play, but not much because the clothes just didn't match, plus I couldn't go to concerts and things like others. I remember my 6th grade class had all decided to get outfits alike for a Christmas party. The guys would get black baggies and white shirts and the girls would also match. I remember mother buying me a pair of baggy pants with the double belt just like all the others, but no shirt. I was too sharp with my yard sale shirt that looked as if I was still in the early 60's and although I was humiliated by others I made it through. So now I'm running with my cousin but we are going to 2 different schools and my school ain't nothing nice. It's the school where the project boys went and where my family lived wasn't too much better. It was all housing authority living. I was a little intimidated because these guys in the 6th grade were jumping other guys and beating them like grown men because although in the 6th grade many of them were older because of getting sent to juvenile detention center or simply just failing or they just looked like grown men. It's sad to say that many of those guys are dead or doing time. Although, I was smart, I only did enough to keep my parents off of my back. Rushing home every day to dance to music from the TV before BET, MTV, and VH1, there was just a music channel that eventually started to show these recorded performances of stars singing and rapping and they were introducing music videos. Shucks, I can remember the summer of 1982 when they began to knock on doors asking if we were interested in this new thing called cable TV. Wow, it was more than just the basic channels, but these stations had profanity, strong sexual content and violence. All the things you can see on regular TV now. So I would come home to sing and dance in the mirror really working hard because, even though I didn't have the best of clothes and hardly kept a fresh hair cut, I could dance better than many. I could use my dancing ability to gain popularity and my cousin could dance also. I figured since I'm running with him maybe they will overlook my hair lining and my ugly gear. So I'm hanging with my cousin, who is popular. He's fighting and breaking into houses and most of all he's having sex. Now at this point, I'm back and forward from West Memphis to Marion because, in Marion, I'm closer to being viewed as normal. In West Memphis, I was viewed as below average, but when I was with my cousin I got certain looks. Some of fear and some of respect, depending on where we were and who was around, but I was good now. Then that all changed. One day in the spring of 1984 me, my uncle his friends and my cousin we were all in Marion and I was 14 then and my cousin and I are talking and he says "I'm about to go to West Memphis". My grandmother heard him and asked where I was going I said I'm going to West Memphis with my cousin. She said No and I knew better than to question her so I said nothing. That was a Saturday and on Monday there was breaking news of a brutal Triple murder and my Cousin was being arrested for that murder. The one I was running with, dancing with, getting a few props with, was pulled from his 8th grade classroom handcuffed and placed in a car live on TV never to see freedom again in his life. Actually, he died in prison. At one time, he was the youngest man in the country on death row. I remember thinking, "I wonder what would have happened to me if I had been there". This was devastating, to say the least, and a fear gripped me because they said that his family was now in danger. I remember being followed by a van of strange people on more than one occasion and hurrying to go to someone's house until they pulled off. Now, I don't know if they wanted me but given the nature of the situation, I was taking no chances. I was on my own again, and truthfully there were people all around me, but I was a misfit even more so a social misfit who didn't know how to initiate a friendship. Those that I did initiate, I always felt inferior because even though we were in the same neighborhood, I always saw that they had more than I did and it was frustrating. Eventually, I found another group of misfits who were from the projects and began skipping school and failing in my grades. School became basically something that I cared nothing for and I decided to skip as much as I could without missing too many days where it would cause my parents to take notice. Eventually, I got caught skipping and my father ended my junior high skipping school career and I decided to get more involved and I tried out for the basketball team. I mean my father was an athlete and he talked about it so much I felt pressure to attempt to become an athlete. I would hear him talk repeatedly about his scholastic career and sports and needless to say the day of the cut with everyone running to see if they made the cut I reluctantly approached the sheet. I waited on everyone to see first and then I looked, I didn't make it. I always felt that I didn't make it because I was too short, but there were guys my height and shorter that made it because they were simply more athletic. I had to face that. As my eighth grade year began to progress, I was basically frustrated and bitter. Getting cut from the basketball team scarred me deeply. I was literally going to the roughest school in the city and I was all alone! And feeling a little intimidated until one day, in PE class, I was playing ball and I was fouled but not bad, but this day I was just fed up and I, at the time, had been taking boxing lessons on the weekends and over the summers with my dad's friend. I was about ready to test my skills and being so mad and bitter because the guy holding me just so happens to be the last guy who made the cut on the basketball team. He basically took my spot right! So I tell him that if he fouls me again we gone have problems. He didn't believe me. He fouled me and I swung and he caught a good one, and just to show you what kind of school I was in, the coach said, "SQUARE OFF"! In other words go ahead and fight and for the second time in my life I sensed that feeling of POWER AND AUTHORITY. Anxious to show my boxing skills I squared off and put em' up and as we circled around I would stick and move, stick and move jab,jab,jab! Oohwee he didn't want no more. I'm literally boxing the crap out of him, yet unfortunately he is one of the PROJECT BOYS and they vowed to get me, but NEVER DID. I think they were all shocked that I had whipped him with no problem and some started to actually talk to me, but still didn't give me the respect I so desired. With my new found glory, I decided to go to my parents at the end of the school year and ask if I could go back to school in Marion because I felt it was a better fit. I had a better shot at girls and being popular. My uncle was a star football player and I had a whole lot of family there, so I convinced them to allow me to live with my grandmother or should I say my Madea. We so affectionately called her. I started to hang out with my uncle on weekends, of course in places neither one of us had any business being in. Even though we were in the country, we had some pretty girls out there. I was hanging out and feeling good. Hanging in the clubs or juke joints that my grandmother despised, I got a chance to show off my superior dance skills, which eventually led to me forming a dance group and entering the talent show and winning 1st place. We made the front page of the local newspaper! Now that's popularity and being noticed like that filled a void that I had been longing for and now since I was gaining a little name for dancing, I thought I was ready to leave the country and go back to West Memphis and try out my new found fame!

Now I'm back after winning a talent show and making the paper and it's all good. I'm the man… Not! But life is about to take a drastic change for the better and the worst. I was reintroduced to my cousins and I remember seeing them a time or two before this and I also remember hearing about them and how they were pretty rough around the edges, and as I began to hang with my cousin and his friends, I meet others in the process. We were running the streets, getting high and meeting girls. We decided to start us a singing/rap group. We even had a manager and began to do shows on the local scene dancing and singing and really gaining popularity. Now another door has opened and I found out that I have the ability to rap. I mean, I could go on for minutes and minutes off the top of my head and it would all make sense. So we stopped singing and started rapping and eventually formed a group called S.I.R. and somehow we started our own record label. We were on a roll and by this time we are hanging out doing all kinds of foolishness and not getting caught. I mean we were out there scrapping every chance we got and we were gaining respect. We would fight anywhere! And that made all the difference, but by this time my mother was tired of all of the fighting. At one time, there was a known killer who said he was going to kill me. So in the summer of 1987 my mother decided to send me to live with my uncle in Nashville to get my life together and I did. I stayed for a couple of weeks, my uncle was friends with the dean of a college and even though I didn't graduate the 12th grade because I missed too many days, I remember being called to the office and I cursed and threatened office personnel and they said leave and never come back! However they had a program that I could get in and finish my 12th grade credits and could began my college courses. I said yes. The weekend before I was supposed to start, I asked could I go home and then come back to start school and they said yes, but I never returned to start school, I decided to run the streets with my boys. I didn't go back home. I would spend the night with my cousin and sometimes even slept on park benches just to say I was on my own. Now hanging with my cousins and we were running the streets and packing pistols but never had to squeeze the trigger. We were fighting and brawling everywhere we went. We were looking for trouble literally, at games, at the movies, and in the streets, we were showing out every chance we got and people respected us. I must say, that kind of respect is intoxicating.

It creates a hunger for more and more and you will almost do anything to prove you deserve it. It's amazing how society will glorify gangstas in films like the Godfather and Scarface. We were infatuated with the gangsta lifestyle and how they had the power and influence and a large portion of the young men in Urban America really wanted that power and influence. Well, somehow my cousin ended up getting arrested for armed robbery and going to prison. Unlike the last time, I wasn't alone. I had my boys and we are about to turn it up a notch. Me, my brother Eric, Len and our DJ WC started to go forward, but the music business was difficult to break into because at that time we had no one from Arkansas in the business. We had to mix and mingle with the Memphis rappers who many went on to make it big like Eight Ball & MJG, SMK, Gansta Pat, Ska-Face Al Kapone! I never figured that part out, but I guess you can say true destiny will interrupt the falseness in your life. We started to get do a lot of shows and recording in the studio. We were destined to be the next big thing from out of Memphis, even though we were from Arkansas.

Then we hooked up with another group and now we were the rap group S.I.R. It consisted of me and my boy Len and brothas of the New World headed by our patna from the big apple and a duo called 2RN (two real niggas) that consisted of my little brother and our patna BK, who was a known Gangsta from West Town. He once shot a guy and then went to the hospital to finish the job! We formed an alliance called H.O.H the HALL OF HELL. We started to do shows and other things. Some things that went on me, Len and others never got involved in things like rape. We were all in for robbery, fighting and shooting. I remember we had dancers in the group and one was being harassed by a college basketball star. She told Len and he called me. We went to the college, took a rubber hammer, and locked this cat up in the stairway. We beat him down, broke his fingers and all. We, unfortunately, ended his career. Then we went home, changed, and went back to the school to see how bad he was hurt! We were jackin people for their cell phones and stealing cars with rims. We even tried to sell them back to the people we stole them from! How gangsta was that! We did it all. Drive bys and everything, we were out of control. One thing I always think about is how my boy Len, who was involved with this life of crime and utter foolishness, would be all in the streets and still kept a job and finished college! That escapes me! But now things are about to take another drastic turn. One day I received a phone call and it was my patna from New York. He is in a New York state of mind, whatever that means. He tells us of a stain we could make. That's hood terminology for robbery. He was giving me all of the details but something just didn't sound right and I didn't know what it was. Something in me was very uneasy about going and there was never a time that I would say no to going but this time I was just feeling different. So I said man it doesn't sound right. Little did I know that he had called everyone else and only myself, another patna and my brother didn't go.

About one hour later, I was doing something and I heard the TV interrupt a show with breaking news that there had been a shooting and two people had died.

Another was shot but survived! The cops were on us and even though I wasn't involved my name came up during questioning. The cops were tapping our phones and tracing our calls doing whatever they could to catch my boys. Now I'm going to speak very candidly about this matter because over the years, I was told that I was a snitch and I turned them in, which couldn't be farthest from the truth! I told my patnas to get out of town because the cops were hot on their trail and I told them that while on the phone. I kept hearing sounds that made me aware of the phone being tapped so I tell them both to get out of town and not to call. One of them decides he would wait on some money to come in the mail. HUH!!! And the other escapes and gets out of town but guess what? He calls and a week later. He's in jail. Now how can I snitch? First, I wasn't there and secondly, I wasn't up on charges so why would I do that! It makes no sense. So now that they are in jail and Len had long decided to make a great decision to move away to start his life and career. My brother and I decided to get a little deeper in the streets. We took on the name H.O.H, added Big L and my boy Big Dog, and started to record a serious album. However, we also began to sell drugs and while we were selling drugs, we purchased cellphones. In our area, we were some of the first people to have cell phones. We were literally balling and now we had the cars with the gold grills. We had the G-ride, 67 dodge with the 2inch whitewalls and chrome wheels. It had dual exhaust with a 15in woofer in the trunk. It was beating down the block we would say. We were in one shoot out after the other, and we would literally write songs about the things that were taking place in our lives because, to us, that was more radical and bold. To tell real stories, about shootings, robberies etc... It was a way for us to gain credibility as gangsta rappers and possibly sell millions of records, but the only problem is you can't rap it and live it. You must make a choice! And we hadn't. I remember the record execs paying for a studio session that my brother and I couldn't make because we were in jail for terroristic threatening. We missed rehearsals for shows because we were in jail for assault. We actually wanted the respect from the streets more than we wanted respect from the rap game. At least that's what our actions said loud and clear.

So as a result of rapping real life stuff, we made a lot of enemies and of course we're selling drugs and robbing folks, so we don't trust none of our surroundings. We are literally paranoid from the drug selling and the shoot outs, but acting as if we can't stop. As I mentioned before, it's intoxicating to have people fear you and even if they don't, just the fact that they know you will do something foolish at any given moment, felt just as good. However, things would begin to take a drastic change in my life because I was involved with so much foolishness and not really considering the fact that I have children. One night while driving, someone that I had previously had a fight with and a couple of shootouts actually tried to shoot me with my daughters in the car. I can remember thinking I don't want my daughters to get hurt. So I began to drive fast and he chased me. I went to the only place that I felt would stop my children from being hurt and I hurried to the police station, even though me and cops didn't get along. I would've done anything to protect my children. I'm happy to say we escaped and the shooter kept going.

Now it wouldn't be long before there was another attempt made on my life. Truthfully, when you are out there in the streets doing all these unlawful and devious things you, never really think. You never really consider that someone other than you could get hurt and that you are actually putting any and everyone that is close to

you in danger. I could've had my mother or father in the car. I could've had my grandparents in the car or I could've been standing outside at their home talking with all my little cousins on the inside and had an attempt on my life. That could've easily turned into the death of an innocent bystander. Hindsight is always 20/20 because looking back I say Whew! I'm glad none of my people got hurt.

THE EXODUS

(THE EXIT)

I never did finish school so I'm marked to be broke and stuck, that's what's up.
I think I'm a get some dope and stand on the corner and press my luck.

Lyric from the song "Raised in the Hood"

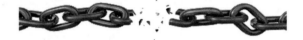

At this point, I will begin to show you those life lessons that will help you to overcome the hood and will help you to believe in yourself and cause you to pursue your destiny.

Throughout many of my experiences it has been made evident that with zero expectations of God to move in a situation, he will surprisingly prove Himself ever present in the forward movement of your destiny. My former statement comes with an express intent to let you know just how involved in your life God will be whether you acknowledge His presence or deliberately ignore the call and the and assignment he has for you.

I am certain there are many instances where feats, some might find trivial or small, can be attributed to God's hand. These feats are those that might otherwise go unnoticed and leave way for minimal, if any, praise by some. I'm referring to something as simple as making it to work on time when you know you should have been late, or perhaps you were unexpectedly distracted and ran a red light. When you look up you feel the rush and see, in your rearview mirror, the passing flash of an 18 wheeled big rig missing you by fractions of an inch.

As the surreal feeling of cognizance washes over you there is an immediate desire or sense to give thanks as a spirit of gratefulness begins to overtake you. There is no mistaking that God's will had been imposed into that situation to further your ability to fall in line with GODS will. These situations are what many cling to for the furthering or building of a relationship with God.

I'd like to think I would have been so open to receiving Gods instructions when I was younger. Being hard headed and head strong in my personal pursuits, I wasn't even remotely looking for any signs that God was talking with me. So what happens when you're not paying attention to God? He talks a little louder to grab your attention.

There are many instances that I had to go through to get on the right path. Fall of 1990 is when I started to engage the dope game i had a patna who had a cousin pushing dope. I knew plenty of people selling drugs and on drugs but again, I never wanted to be that guy. I got behind on my bills and that's never a good look for anyone trying to find his place in manhood. My patna's cousin told me to give him one hundred dollars. So I did. I took what he gave me for the hundred dollars and sure enough I made two hundred and fifty dollars. It was the beginning of easy money. It was the beginning of a long stretch of victimization upon my own community with little regard for the consequences. There were few studies that depicted the overall effects of drug abuse. There were even fewer outlets in my community shining a light on the matter. With a clear conscience and a clear plan for my come up, I set out to get me a piece of this easy money world.

We would serve rocks to people and the exchange was the whole point. There were cats out there that would take anything as long as they felt like they had come up a little. I mean it was cats willing to accept TV's, jewelry, sexual favors, or whatever they saw value in. We didn't want your busted TV's, VCRs, or stereos... none of that.

We know what we selling. We know how bad you want it. So this is what we will do for you. Okay you don't have money right now. But you will on the 1st and 15th. So I'll front you this $20.00 rock and on the first you owe me $100 in interest. When you have a product that creates its own demand solely on being what it is. We really could charge $300 interest. It would have worked for a bit, but that would have really eaten into budgets and made people think they could hide out and dip on paying. That would have only lead to physical confrontation and a whole other kind of existence we didn't want to deal with.

So on the 1st and 15th we were really racking in easy money like you wouldn't believe. Coming up on a few thousand dollars was really easy to do. Getting rid of it doing whatever, whenever was just as easy to do. Just when you thinking it can't get any easier life will show you just how wrong you are. At the same time, I've already stated there is no such thing as easy money. So when the police lights come on and we know we ain't done nothing, today, we keep going. My brother and I hit the corner and cut a left. They are right behind us and they cut a left too. We hit the corner and cut another left thinking let's get out of these fools way. They hit the corner and boom cut another left.

Now I'm thinking it's about to be some mess. They just want to harass us because they might have heard something about what we got going on. We pull over get our license and registration and they come up to the car. The window is down and they play it cool. They go through the regular script and we play along. Knowing we haven't done anything and knowing that the car is clean I really kind of got a problem. I wanted to know what we were being pulled over for. Basically, running through their script and checking our I.D. was more or less to confirm we were who they were looking for.

Dirty cops are worse than criminals on the street. They take minimal risk and the majority of the profits. These cats decided they would give us an opportunity to sell drugs for them. They wanted to welcome us to the dope game on a higher level. That easy money looked us right in the face and smiled. If I didn't know anything in all my life, I knew the boys in blue protect the boys in blue. We laughed it off while playing dumb. We gave the impression that we assumed they were joking and that we had nothing to do with the selling of any drugs.

After all when you get in too deep there is no such thing as crawling out of the hole.

When the police put you in a hole you're officially in too deep. They're watching you to ensure the adequate handling of their money and to cover their tails. If they're watching you they're keeping records and if they're keeping records its' really only a matter of time before those records come to light. Who can dispute police records? Those cats knew we were lying. They didn't care. We didn't care how serious they were.

Dealing with the police would have been a death sentence, whether it was a physical death or a more spiritual one where we became their errand boys. It would have never been as glamorous as they tried to make it out to be. We dodged that bullet and potentially so many more. Besides, selling drugs all month and collecting on the first charging sixty, eighty, one hundred dollars interest was working just fine.

It was Summer of 1992 It was an average day. I wouldn't say there was anything out of the ordinary that would cause for me to be alarmed. My brother and I were walking down the dope track in sunset, serving fiends left and right. We were doing what we do, getting money and talking about getting money. Across the street, coming from the opposite direction, was a local hustler, that goes by the name of T- money. He's dapper; his crew is all in the dope game or wants to be. They are tagging along for the sake of hood fame alone. As he got closer I could hear him yell, "Der go dat nigga K. W. (Dubya) right there!

Nigga, I heard y'all put a headhunter out on me. Y'all trying to get somebody to do me in?"

Between making his way across the street and being in my presence, he saw fit to acquire one of those bars people use to link vehicles together when towing. Keep in mind; I wasn't exactly being quiet as he first made his way towards me. We had a harsh exchange of words that told me this situation was escalating quickly before he made it to my side of the street; I ran into the house and grabbed a shotgun. Yes, it was loaded. No, I wasn't considering the ramifications of my actions.

Now, back outside with the gun in his face, the situation was so far past the point of no return, I'd surely need a passport to travel back the great distance to find it. I should have kept going. I could have kept going. When I ran into the house I should have run out the back door and through the neighborhood. As much as I'd like to think that was an option, I know wholeheartedly it wasn't. My brother was out there. My home was now the scene of the incident. I definitely couldn't run away, being who I was back then, there was a certain expectation for those living my lifestyle. To do what I

was doing, how I was doing it, respect was as necessary a tool as the drugs I was selling and the guns I was carrying. To be honest, the respect really had to be more prominent than the rest. It almost made the guns obsolete. Those who respected you knew the gun was around. They knew the gun was a factor in any situation.

It was the select few, who didn't respect you despite your reputation, who made the gun necessary. On this day, I was about to extend my level of respect throughout the neighborhood. With this gun in his face and my finger on the trigger, everything else was tuned out. I could see down the stretch of the barrel. My finger tip gripped the receiver with sweaty palms and ill intentions. To this day I can still smell the oil used to clean the gun. I can still hear the deafening crowd forming. Above all else I can hear T- moneys bravado.

I'm the one with the gun. I am the one who should be barking at him, but we're both still verbally lashing out at one another. Considering T-money was as much a product of my environment as I was, he had a reputation to uphold as well. He is glaring down this barrel towards me without showing the slightest bit of fear. I guess he figured since he is about to die no one would say he turned soft in the midst of his final moments. No matter his demeanor, with no regard for the crowd I stood strong.

He is supposed to back down. He is supposed to surrender and show me the respect he didn't when he first arrived. He doesn't, instead as we argue he seems to grow in confidence. His bravado matches my own as my eyes shift and I see my father has joined the crowd. My mother has joined the crowd as well as my grandfather who we called Papaw. The neighborhood was out and it has now become a spectacle. T-money, more than likely, felt confident that I was not willing to go the distance. Out of the confusion, he stares down the barrel and utters the most pathetic words, "Nigga, you scared to shoot."

First you come to my street, my house, and my face accusing me of putting a hit out on you when I have never been afraid to handle my own business as needed. Then you disrespect me by running up on me with a pipe. A crowd forms and you think you have the upper hand because of some unrealistic idea of who you think I am? You know they say a bull sees red and he charges. I've since learned that it's not the red that attracts the bull, but the motion of the matador's cape that coaxes the bulls actions. I am not a bull. I saw red. I felt an unspeakable rage and I pulled the trigger with no regard for him or any other collateral damage.

He saw me pull the trigger. He saw the jerk of the shotgun. Then he saw my face and my resolve when the gun DIDN'T fire. He didn't have time to be grateful. I hit him with the barrel of the gun and the fight ensued. His pipe found its way to my head. He was strong. I mean this was definitely a fight for my life. As blood ran down we fought tooth and nail. I can't fully recall what ended the fight, but I know I never got a second chance to pull that trigger. His face was mangled, my head was busted, and the hand of God saved me, saved us.

In retrospect, God saved a great many people by that single incident alone. I could have been a murderer. My children would have no father, my parents would have lost a son, and my sister and brother would have lost a sibling.

I know the gun was loaded. I know the gun was clean. I know the hammer slammed into the charge. No doubt there was an indention in the bed of the cartridge.

Nothing short of God stopping me from becoming a murderer to ensure I fell in line with His will is what took place on that day. As I laid there bleeding profusely, T-money and his crew had fled the scene. My grandfather's face was visibly dissatisfied through the blood in my eyes. My grandfather tried to talk to me. In my mind, it was the wrong time. In my mind all I could think about was the gun didn't fire even though I pulled the trigger.

I heard Papaw's voice. I saw his face and his words fell on a non-receiving heart. He kneeled down and tried to speak sensibly. Being a soft-spoken man, most anything he said could be considered as said sensibly. "Kevin, man, I'm tired of y'all coming around here acting a fool. Y'all gone have to stop before somebody gets killed."

I cursed him out without hesitation. In so many words, I explained to him how I didn't start this. I made it clear he needed to get away from me because he didn't understand the world we were living in. After all, T-money and his crew had brought the trouble to me. I had every right to defend myself when they came to me. There were two things you definitely didn't do that you'd never live down. One, you don't back down from anyone, anywhere ever. Two, you don't show fear while standing your ground. That is the quickest way to lose any ground you may have. T-money and I both upheld the dumbest standards in a situation that held absolutely no significance in existence.

Or at least, I felt at that time there was no significance. I'm reminded of the story of Joseph when I think about this particular incident. Long before it was stated in Romans 8:28 and we know that all things work together for good to them that love God, to them who are the called according to his purpose. Joseph's brothers sold him into slavery. Undoubtedly, this was an atrocious act that leads to a great deal of hurt and distress. Without that very action having taken place, Joseph would have never been on the path that leads him to interpreting the

Pharaoh's dream, allowing him to save the many people of Egypt from the coming drought, become Governor, or provide for his family that had cast him away.

Even though I wasn't operating on the love for God that I could have been, working with a full understanding of his inner workings in my life, or working on my relationship with him, we serve a God who is Alpha and Omega. He knows the beginning and the ending. So I believe his foresight into my future love for Him, coupled with the praying family members who covered me in the midst of my foolishness, gave way to him moving on my behalf in many instances, this one in particular.

My life eyes were opened in this incident, having had over a dozen staples and a new permanent line in my head. I sat back and reflected as I healed. Even though I wasn't listening at the time, I heard every word my grandfather had said. Somebody was going to get killed. It could have been me. It could have been one of the random people who had gathered in the crowd. It could have been my brother, mother, or father. One of T-money's boys could have pulled out a gun that didn't misfire and ended any chance of me aligning myself with God's will. A change was coming, but it wasn't coming soon enough. It wasn't long after that incident with T-money that I found myself in the studio recording yet another hood classic. My brother, a few of our patnas were just finishing up and leaving the studio.

Across from our exit, there was a group of fellas minding their own business. They had a few girls hemmed up on the corner. They were spitting some serious game. I don't remember if the women looked nice or not. All I know is we felt like being us and who we were was a couple guys who did what we wanted. So we yell out, "Aye, can we holla too!" They could have been married, they could have been dating; we didn't know and didn't care. We casually strolled on to our vehicle. Of course, the men were enraged. An argument ensued. The colorful language could have painted the ceiling of the Sistine Chapel ten times over.

We get into our car and ride out. These dudes decide they aren't done talking so they hop in their vehicle and pursue us. I'm driving and I see this. I am not the least bit concerned because that would have meant they presented themselves as a threat, they hadn't. I'm driving and they pull up beside us yelling out the window. I know we're going somewhere between fifty and sixty miles an hour. Its late, the streets are empty so we roll down the windows and yell back at them.

My brother and patnas, now hanging out the windows yelling and cussing and telling them what they ain't gone do and how they don't know us and how much we don't care about what they have to say. Equally speeding down the highway, they're not hanging out the car, but their windows are down and they have no clue what kind of monsters they're being disruptive with. One of the young men figured he would show us just how serious they were and show us just how much we didn't know whom we were messing with. He flashes a handgun with a look in his eyes, daring us to back down. It was all I could do to keep my composure. It's one thing to talk trash and call us names; it is another thing all together to threaten our lives over a few curse words.

I've never claimed to be any sort of big bad wolf, but I've always had the wherewithal to know when to escalate things past my own security being at risk. Without hesitation or thought, we pulled out guns. I hit the brakes and my crew already knew what that meant. The sound of our screeching tires filled the night's air. The scent of rubber burning singed our nostrils. As our top speed came to a halt, the dust and debris from our abrupt stop could be seen twisting and twirling behind the car.

I could feel my heart in my chest as I heard the guys with me open fire on the opposing vehicle. The clinking of steel and clattering of slugs and shell casings falling where they may, gave me an ambivalent sense of self. I believe Swiss cheese would adequately depict the end scene of that vehicle. I'd be lying if I said I remember them firing a single shot back at us. No one in the vehicle was killed or hurt past their pride, but the message was very clear. We didn't know those dudes from Adam, but as the streets go, somehow word got out.

It didn't take very long before we were all questioned by the police about the incident that occurred on the highway. There was no booking or charges pressed. It was really just another random day in the hood. In most cases, I can now look back and clearly see God's presence. I don't think there could be a more direct *juxtaposition* that this event would correlate with than the story of the fiery furnace. Everything in me tells me that there is no reason those men should have survived being under fire of that magnitude. The car was a shell of its former self. God sent his angel to protect those men in that car as much as he sent them to protect those in mine.

Again, we could have been murderers. We could have spent the rest of our lives in jail or on death row. I can't express to you enough how important it is to consider God in ALL your ways. We cannot be led by our emotions and driven to act without clear consideration of the ramifications of our actions. It can very well lead to the devastation and destruction of your family. I can't speak to the level of faith those men had. I can't speak to the level of faith of any other man in the car with me. But I know God chose to intervene and save all of us from ourselves.

The car drove off, we drove away. We headed home and the whole encounter became a memory that would later show me one of many instances God called me to him and I ignored his voice. At this point, I was listening though. At this point I wasn't entirely canceling him out. I knew something was happening in my life, but I wasn't fully aware of what it was. Shadrach, Meshach, and Abednego came out of that furnace unscathed, even when the men who took them to it perished upon arrival.

Many people like to focus on the fact that they came out without a blemish or burn. I don't take anything away from that. It is a prominent story that holds great weight within the kingdom. It's value for going through struggles and knowing that God will be with you in the midst of the worst-case scenario is a tried and true testament to His power. But when I look back at that incident I think about how the three boys were taken to the furnace and those who wished to put them into the worst of it perished. Now considering His power was so great that he could save them in the midst, surely he could have saved them from having had to go into it in the first place. Their escorts perished from the heat alone. But no, no they fell into the furnace anyway.

Shadrach, Meshach, and Abednego had a destiny to fulfill and that destiny included going where those who wished them harm couldn't go, even when the destination was of their own design. I believe it was never meant for us not to start that confrontation. It was never meant for us not to escalate it to the point that we did. Just as Shadrach,

Meshach, and Abednego stood in that fire and showed Nebuchadnezzar there was nothing he could say or do to remove the power of the God they served, I had to experience life in such a manner to reach those who don't have the same call upon their lives that I do.

Someone had to be on the front line. Someone had to take the hits. Someone had to make the mistakes and be pulled out like a child in breached birth in order to live and show those still drowning in the midst of their personal turmoil that there is a life past the streets. There is a way of existence outside of easy money. Easy money usually equates to easy funerals or hard jail time. Easy money is very alluring. When you say it the words just sound sexy. The words feel sexy as they begin in the back of your throat and drift past your lips and it sounds even better.

The problem with easy money is that it's literally an oxymoron. Money is a current medium of exchange. To exchange means to move or transfer from one place to another for something in return, essentially putting in work. To work means exactly that. Do something other than nothing. And we have to work to get money. We have to work to get that exchange to take place. When it is easy and you cut corners on working, you cut corners on the benefits of the exchange.

The benefit of the exchange is where you break it down into whether or not the money is easy or clean. The allure of easy money is what brought me to my first encounter with selling drugs. At first, I never wanted to be that guy. You know the guy who sells drugs to other people, but the pressures of life and the easy access to it made it so easy to fall victim in my surroundings.

I know what you're thinking. I made a choice to start and I made a choice to continue just like I made a choice to stop. How could I consider myself falling victim? Without a long and exhaustive explanation I'll just say that within the realm of the social hierarchy I was born into, being under the covering of those who came before me and having grown up in a world where I was viewed as a problem before I was viewed as a man, the victimization was evident and daunting. I fell into it. I didn't see any other option. I had made decisions that left me with fewer options than those who had made all the right decisions and were still struggling.

July 1993, my life was literally out of control and I was tired. I couldn't get a break in the music industry, I was fighting and shooting and I was being shot at with my daughters in the car!! How crazy is that? On top of that, I was in a marriage that I didn't respect and had girls on the side and everything! Well I eventually got a job because things were so hectic and I was receiving phone calls from prison that the cops had me and my brother's names on a list for drug trafficking and truthfully we were offered by a kingpin to transport drugs for him. One day while we were in jail, we decided not to do it. We were selling drugs, but not enough to be on a list and honestly, I believe it was the violence that made them think we were deeper in the game than we actually were. I mean we knew people and we had favors out there and family who was heavy and not to mention we sold dope all through the night while living across the street from a sheriff who literally hated my guts!!!! In looking back, I can't really blame him!!!

I have now been working a job as a Security Guard and It was pretty consistent and I believed I was doing better. I was an unarmed guard, but I was still packing and one day I had a real light bulb moment! I noticed that the residents at the apartments that I worked at would always have certain visitors on the 1st and 3rd of the month. Obviously drug dealers and so I called my brother and told him we are about to Nino Brown (new jack city) this spot next month and I started bringing my own drugs to work and I would charge ridiculous interest 60-80 bucks on a 20 dollar rocks. It would be like taking candy from a baby.

So now I have been selling drugs the whole month and I see the mail man coming. I know he is about to deliver the checks!!! Then drug dealers started to come to the complex to do business, but since they had to come through me I wouldn't let them in. I reserved the right to keep people out if I suspected any funny business and it was obvious these guys were drug dealers!!! And I got to do my job. Well I would eventually lose my job and therefore I could no longer play Nino Brown. So now we in the streets doing whatever, whenever.

But I remember God really trying to get my attention and I not listening. I proceeded to try to be a drug dealer with a conscience, in other words, I used to sell drugs to anyone and charge ridiculous interest on my drugs. I now would not charge ridiculous interest on men and women with children, in fact if they had children I would not give them much credit (how righteously unrighteous is that!!!) because I didn't want the children to suffer, at my expense. Eventually I stopped selling drugs, got another job, and tried to fly straight, well straight according to my rules. I was still hoping to break into music and I was no longer selling drugs. I just decided I would smoke a little weed and that I wouldn't bother anyone and just kinda keep to myself. Next would be a series of events that would take my life spiraling downward and me making some tough, but intelligent decisions. I was getting off work one Friday, I had just gotten paid and I called my cousin, the weed man, and bought me a quarter of weed. I was going to stop at the local store and get me some swishers and go home and get high all alone. As I was pulling up to the store, I noticed the police behind me and I get out I look to the left at another building and I saw another cop. Then I looked to the right and across the street and I realized I was surrounded by cops. I go in the store to stall. I was thinking, "What do they want." Truthfully, it could have been a laundry list of things that had just caught up with me. I was in the store; I bought some chips and some motor oil so I can take the weed out of my pocket and stuff it in my motor. I was thinking that whatever they want, I don't want to get caught with weed in my pocket too. I come out and I pop the hood and then

I took my oil cap off and stuffed the weed down in there and began to pour oil on top and suddenly the cops swooped in and rushed me. They told me I was under arrest! While they're handcuffing me, I constantly asked what I did, why are you arresting me and they would just reply we don't have to tell you anything. And now I was thinking this is it. We arrived to the police station and when they opened the cell there was my brother and my cousin also in jail. We had no clue why? At least my brother and I don't, so finally they told us we were charged with battery and they were working on upgrading it to attempted murder!!! Well here is what happened, there was an argument in my neighborhood the night before with two guys and one of them was my cousin and my cousin pulled out his pistol and began to shoot. While he was shooting the guy, the girl took off running. When the cops arrived they told them it was the Whitakers, which automatically brought my brother and I into the mix. We were not there though!! We had no knowledge of the incident!! So we went to court and my cousin had agreed to tell the judge that we weren't there and had nothing to do with the shooting. The judge politely told him to shut up and set bond at $50,000 dollars and back to jail we went!! I was sitting in jail thinking about all the stuff I had done. I was in jail facing time for something I didn't do. How crazy is that! It taught me that karma is real and eventually what you do will catch up with you.

So as we sat in jail I asked to speak to the detective working the case who was my boy Len's uncle. He knew me so they agreed and took me to his office and he asked me, "Kevin did you do it?" I replied I didn't and told him if he would think back that every time they picked me up, I never denied anything that I had actually done! So why would I now. He said to me can anyone verify you were at home! I said yes!!! And he said who? I said, "The sheriff was home and he saw me in my yard at the time they said that the shooting took place!!!" He said, "Ok then we will question him." Initially the sheriff said he didn't see me and here I am sitting in jail without proof to back up my story and after several days and praying to

God, the detective then sent for me and said that the sheriff came back and said he did remember seeing me in the in the yard. As soon as they released my brother, we went back to the concrete jungle (streets). So I go back to my job, but not making enough money to pay my bills. I was a little frustrated. I had responsibilities. I had to pay rent, utilities and take care of my babies. I needed money fast and I knew just how to get it and so I decided to go and get a $50 pack because I knew I could get the hook up from the hood. I did and I got from him what we used to call monkey nuts (large pieces of crack) and after that I decided to go to the store. I got some crackers, cheese spread and a grape soda and I'm headed home. As I got closer to my turn, I saw police lights and I keep going, cuz they got someone pulled over and everything in me told me to go another route, but I didn't. I figured that they wouldn't leave the car they got to pull me over, so I was riding. Me, my cheese and crackers, grape soda, and a loaded 357 were headed home and as I passed the cops they noticed my car and left the car they had and began to follow me and they turned their lights on, but I kept going trying to figure it out what to do with the gun. Finally, I thought to myself, unload the gun and throw the bullets out because an empty gun is not that serious. After I did, I pulled over. The cops began to search the car and the found the gun, which they never charged me with, and I had my drugs in my mouth and I was chewing it like gum and trying to swallow, but I began to choke on the plastic. As they turned me around, I threw the crack. Unfortunately, they saw me and they stayed out there for hours until they found it. However, I had chewed it up so bad that they thought it was powder and I was a user not a dealer and everyone knows that is a lesser charge. They locked me up and the next day I bailed out, but had a court date. So now things began to take a serious turn for the worst. Normally, when you are attempting or contemplating a change, the devil will throw things your way to derail you or change the thoughts you have to better yourself. One evening, while sitting in my living room, I hear shots ring out and my slide door to the patio shattered. I jumped up and ran outside screaming bloody murder. I see a car pulling off and it wasn't anyone that I had a problem with, at least as far as I knew. When you live life on the edge you never know who you have offended or hurt, sometimes innocently.

So I did what all others do when trouble rises, I called the police and when they came they said, "It appears that the shots came from the inside" I said why would I shoot in my own house and I tried to tell them that someone had jumped my fence and shot in the house but they kept implying I did it. Even when they saw the bullets in the wall over the sofa where my two year old daughter was sitting, they still didn't believe me!!

So I called my brother and we decide that tomorrow we would see what the problem was!! We got up early with drama on our mind and we decide to grab the sawed off and go ask a few questions. When we hit the block there he was the guy who did the drive by on my home, but the problem is that he's riding with a childhood friend. I know he had absolutely nothing to do with the drama, but I cannot miss the opportunity to confront the issue. He is in the wrong place at the right time with the wrong person and I gotta deal with it. I approached the vehicle and opened the door and asked him why he shot at my house. He began to reach under the seat, I swung and hit him and the driver, who was scared to death, hit the accelerator. They went in reverse. I was caught in the door and my brother jumped out of the car screaming "Die nigga die". He hit the pump and the windshield shattered everywhere!!! We sped off and now we are on the run and he heard that the driver was rushed to the hospital because buck shots hit him and eventually, later that day, we turned ourselves in and went ahead and got the process started. Initially, fear struck me because out of all the things we had done over the years, this time, I knew it was serious because someone innocent got hurt.

We found ourselves in court for a span of two years or so until we could no longer afford a lawyer. For me, this is where my transformation truly began and all that I was destined to become started to unfold.

I was already up on a drug charge and now I was facing time with this matter. I began to reflect on my life and all I was dealing with. I started to go to church, even though I had grown up in church, I had become so far removed from that and fully dedicated to a life of foolishness. I was going to church and I was angry not really receiving and then one day I decided to pay attention. I heard some things that would began to take my life in a totally different direction. I must admit, it was difficult because as I began to change. I had to change my surroundings and the people I was dealing with. One of those people was my brother, who I love dearly, but I knew if I was going to change I had to make the tough decisions. We went back and forth to court and finally were approaching the day of reckoning. By this time, I had completely turned my life around, however because we were guilty of the crime, I began to prepare myself for prison. I had hoped but never really expected to remain free. I got up that particular morning and I began to think that this was the day I must give an account of my wrong doings, not just that one incident. I truly believed for all that I had done and got away with that this was it. We got to court and it was a long day. Many are going to prison with long sentences and now I was up!! A lot was going through my mind. I was thinking about how my children would feel because I was facing 20 years. They said I had to do 10 flat before I was eligible for parole. Mentally I was ready for a long stay. By this time, we had no lawyer because we had run out of money and the reality of my consequences began to way heavy. The three guys before me had all gotten at least twenty to thirty years and the Judge is looking mean as ever. Obviously he's not having a good day!!! They called my name and I stepped out. The judge does something that is absolutely uncommon. He first informs me that they had been watching me for a while since the incident and they hadn't seen me in the streets. They believed I was a different person than before and he said to me that I was sentenced to a ten year suspended sentence which meant I didn't have to go to jail, but if I got in any trouble I would get the full twenty years. They gave my brother ten years of which he only had to do three.

I was a free man, but not really. I had ten years' probation for the felony drug charge, ten year suspended sentence and several thousands of dollars in fines. With all of this baggage began my true transformation.

These events took place at a time when I was reaching a critical and pivotal point in my life. It was right before I would fall in full supplication before God and plead with him to remove me from my old ways and allow me to become something new. I had a marriage, children, and family that all could benefit from me being better than who I was.

It was in 1995 that I'm in church on a regular. I'm striving to change my ways and become a new creature. Changing for the better is one of the hardest things to do when all eyes see the former you every day. Accusing eyes can break a man. Accusing tongues can tear him down. It takes a great deal of personal strength to take the lashings of those equally sinful in order to move forward on your own personal journey. I could have lashed back at them. I could have lashed out first, knowing that their judgment was falling on me every time I stepped into the church. It wouldn't have helped me grow as a person. It would serve me better to be the change I hoped to see and hoped they would see rather than give lip service to the ideal I was striving for. As the old saying goes, action speaks louder than words. I had committed myself to living my own personal truth as I began to build my relationship with God.

When you seek to build that relationship with Him, He will certainly allow you the space. There usually comes a point when he does something contrary to the forward movement of that relationship, not for His benefit, but for your furthered growth.

A friend and mentor of mine, Dr. T.C. Maxwell, once wrote, "Words can't tell you who God really is, they can describe His character at points in eternity," from his book Spiritual Warfare. He would liken such points in eternity akin to a snapshot or momentary glimpse at God's omnipresence. He went on to write, "The picture doesn't do Him justice. God Himself must be revealed to your spirit to know Him, only through the Word of God by the Spirit of Truth can we understand even a tiny portion of Him", also from the book Spiritual Warfare. It is with my pursuit of understanding God that I realize even though I was not operating within His will through my actions, His will, his purpose, and his design for my life will win out over my selfish desires.

I implore you to listen to Him, as He welcomes you. When you've reached a point that He has destined for you to grow in Him, you will be tested for your resolve. Such a test came to me as I sought to immerse myself in the church. Once again I'm working and struggling to pay my bills. I'm learning the word and I'm applying it and it just doesn't seem like it's manifesting before me.

I'm making heads way in my faith and I've not only submitted to the church, but also accepted a call on my life. The bills are still piling up. My job isn't paying me much and stress is mounting in my marriage. Along comes a prominent drug dealer doing very well for himself. It's almost unreal when you think about it. Not only was the police watching me, waiting for me to mess up, but the streets were watching too. There is undoubtedly a whole message in that statement alone. The worst part is both are watching for the same reason. That way the decade of probation I'm sitting on can be slapped on me and I waste away behind bars for the best years of my girl's childhood, but here comes this kingpin with his quick, EASY, and certainly life changing for the WORST, money making plan. This cat had the sharpest clothes, the nicest car, and the type of jewelry you see on display. The kind you imagine buying, but would more than likely never get.

One day he comes up to me and immediately I look left then right checking the corners and the cut from every angle trying to see what type of setup this must be. He is, as they used to say, all smiles, walking with a stride you only get when money is far from being a problem. We go through a simple enough greeting and I'm looking at him strong wondering what his agenda is. In the back of my mind, I am immediately standing at a crossroads in my life. This could play out as a simple meet and greet with two free men who once had a mutual respect. This could turn out to be some old trouble I created unaware like with the guy who shot out my side door. Or, this could be a plethora of other things that I don't have time to consider since he's standing right in front of me talking while I'm thinking.

I tune in to catch his words that I have to ask him to repeat. I know he didn't say what I thought he said.

"Come on now, K. W. If you really want to make some money I mean really rake it in. This is the time. You have this nice cover set up. You're in ministry now, you're faithful to the ministry, and you are always on time too. You're the first one there and the last one to leave. It doesn't get any better than that."

I'm just looking at him. Why, no, how does he know all of this. These streets will surprise you from one day to the next. I ask him what he is getting at so we can finish this conversation. I'm living my life and he views it as a cover. At this point I'm as genuinely removed from the dope game and the violence, as anyone would expect the average man to be.

He goes on to explain how I could really camouflage the drug game by being in ministry if I really wanted to do something big. If I really wanted to make some serious money being in ministry was a key element in throwing everyone off my tracks. When I say this temptation he had just sat in my lap was stronger than any woman I had ever come across, I mean every word of it. I was broke. I was struggling. I was trying to do right and not seeing any reward for my actions.

I would never compare myself to Jesus. I am fully aware that I should be His express image as a representation on this earth, but when I think of how this man came in, while I was in the midst of a seemingly forced fast, fasting on money, fasting on love, fasting on hope, fasting on security, fasting on a clear view of my future, here he is like the devil tempting Jesus in the wilderness. With a smile on his face and cheer in his voice at this marvelous idea he is telling me, all I have to do to take over the world is this, that, and the other. If I had been a little less removed from the streets than I probably would have slapped him right in the face with the bible opened to Matthew 4.

As good as it all sounded and as much as I could have used the income this man's proposition would have generated, I had come into the understanding of God's love for me and his reward for the faithful. It isn't my place to question when he moves or how he moves on my behalf, but to trust that he will move. With little to no reluctance at all, I respectfully declined his offer and sent him on his way.

From time to time, I wonder if ever he found a person in the ministry to follow through with his idea of a perfect cover. Nevertheless, I was at my crossroads and I willingly chose Jesus. After all, no one gets to the father except through him right? So I need the father in my life, not only for me, but also for my girls and the longevity of where my life would someday take me.

In the words of the street poet Sean Carter, "I came to a fork in the road and went straight" from the song Renegade. It wasn't an easy decision, but it was the best decision. That path may have been the last straw that left me on the side of the road. It could have been the path that led me to an incident where my daughters didn't survive. Someone could have shot into my home for retaliation or to send a message.

The possibilities for heartache and devastation are endless when you're not living in God's will and even when you are. At least when you are covered in the blood, you know to pray away those possibilities and be grateful when you see another day, have your health, feel the love of those you surround yourself with, and have the opportunity to spread God's love and word to those who come across your path.

I made a choice to pursue my destiny with God. I made a choice to overcome my former self and strive to create a more complete me, who will be an example to those I meet. I made the choice to show those around me that God's plan involves you and it's up to you to decide whether or not you're going to fall in line with it or ignore the call and fall subject to a probate mind allowing the devil and life to hit you from all angles with no covering.

77

DARK PATHS

I'm living life on the edge but I'm hanging on. But I gotta keep my head high cuz I gotta stay strong!

Lyric from "Can't Hold Me Down"

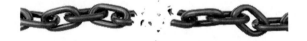

In this chapter, I want to share the struggles that I had to deal with coming into the harsh reality of being a felon with a calling to preach. I was used to being hard, but I was in for a hard journey that could've broken me and left me in pieces. I discovered what it really meant to hold on when there is not much to hold on to! To find that inner strength time and time again so that every time life tries to break you, somehow you hold it together. Even at times when you are falling apart there is something that makes you bounce back. I was reminded of a movie that starred Samuel Jackson and Bruce Willis titled Unbreakable. It was a fictional story that in many ways displayed a very simple truth. It was as if the characters played by the two stars were very different people who represented the same person. One guy was very fragile and weak and every time he fell he was broken. The other was the exact and extreme opposite of him. He was unusually strong and his bones could handle whatever pressure that was applied. He would heal extremely fast. It was a representation of how we are in life. On one hand we are fragile beings on a journey that is uncertain and filled with challenges that are beyond our natural ability. Then, on the other hand, we are stronger than we can imagine. We are tougher than alligators! On my path, I have felt both weak and like I can't be stopped! What ever the case, through it all, I have been too hard to break.

Life became difficult. I was a young man, married, with four children, counting my step daughter and my then wife's niece. I have a lot of responsibility and I was now starting to see that I must begin to shift my life for the better. I needed to do what was necessary to better myself! I was going to church and at the time I had a jerry-curl. Now this is mentioned because where I was from, if you had a jerry curl you were considered more gangsta or more a thug. I had earrings in both ears, not that earrings will send you to hell, I was more so talking of the stigma that comes with a young man in the hood wearing them. I was focused on change and being a better man, but even when you change for the better, everyone is not willing to except the fact that it's a sincere effort for the better. People continued to look at me as the same person that I was. They wouldn't let go of my past. You will find that the hardest people to convince are not strangers but your family at times can become your greatest doubters and naysayers. I had family members saying I would never amount to anything and that I would never change for the better even years after. I had become a completely different person. You cannot allow the opinions of others to become the measuring rule for your destiny. You must fulfill your destiny in spite of those who can't see where you are going.

1995 I am now on probation and the misery of it would weigh on me like a ton of bricks. I would dread going to see my probation officer because; even though I was a different person, they treated me like a common criminal every time I had to report. Eventually, I accepted my call into ministry and I was preaching and on probation and being treated like a thug, cuz they don't care about what you say or what you have become. They believe it's what they call jailhouse salvation, which is basically getting saved because you are in trouble. I want to say to all who may read this book, in jail, on probation, or parole; you must get to a point where you are no longer moved by what people think. You changed because a good change is just good, no matter the motivation. There are more people held in a stagnate place in life because they are simply afraid of what others may think of their efforts to turn it all around! That fear gives people too much power over your purpose.

I was a felon, but I got a job spraying chemicals and actually the boss don't care if I'm a felon or not! I started as a helper making $5.50 an hour and getting 40+ hrs a week. I had a financial turnaround. I was asked to be a driver. Yes, I ran my own truck. One problem that I have is that I can't drive a stick. I decided to learn and I did and needless to say I got the position. I'm now training others on the job and the company's business is growing. I was doing my job so well. I began to ask for and receive increases in my hourly wage all the way until I was put on salary. It wasn't easy, but I had a drive I wanted to prove to myself that I could handle. I must admit it wasn't easy, but hard work was in my blood and the will to succeed was in my heart, therefore quitting was not an option. I had to go hard for what I believed God had prearranged for my life. All must get into a relationship with him in order for those plans to be revealed and fulfilled. Here is what we need to understand. All of us have a gift. We have that something that sets us apart from others. That one thing or things that makes you uniquely you. Many times, it's the things that others don't like about you that actually set you apart from others. That thing will bring prosperity into your life. In fact, you connect with God and allow him to show you what to do to prosper in life. I often say that major drug dealers are extremely misguided business men who don't have anyone to nurture their talents. Thieves and crooks are misguided. They should be in the military or starting security companies. Pimps are gifted speakers and salesmen and thugs and brawlers should have been boxers or wrestlers. The truth is, we all are gifted to do something and we must make it our business to find what that is.

In my dark paths, I experienced much rejection, heartache and disappointments; however, in spite of all those things I knew God had something better for me. I knew God would eventually open doors because I was so determined to be better. Basically, being better is a matter of choice. Often people don't move forward because they are afraid to make decisions, to call the shots, but in order for your life to expand beyond the darkness that you are in, you must make better decisions. There is a pivotal moment, a day of reckoning with yourself when you determine if you have what it takes to go high in life. If you have what it takes to soar beyond what you have seen or experienced! Now there were times on my job when I had to rise above some things in order to solidify that I was changed, not just for others, but for myself. I worked with mostly white guys and one day one of them decided to use the word nigger (not nigga). Now he wasn't using it towards me, however it was very disrespectful and I had not learned how to yet confront issues without violence so I sucked it up and said if he is going to be a fool then I wouldn't be one with him. I had a family and things to consider and I knew my future was bright. I couldn't let one idiot stop me from getting to it, because when you are transitioning your life you must challenge yourself to stretch beyond your normal capacity and endeavor to advance and excel. My life was shifting and I had a lot of internal conflict because, even though I had a job and eventually would make pretty good money, I had to get over the thought of making fast money. It was a real test of faith, of believing that you can be a better person. All of my life, as far back as I can remember, my family struggled and the thoughts of getting out there in those streets to make ends meet was a haunting feeling. I will say some things that most preachers will not say. I had a lot of fun in the streets. I didn't leave the streets or the street mentality because weed stop getting me high, or liquor quit getting me drunk. Here is a wow for you; I actually enjoyed the thug mentality. I enjoyed playing by my own rules or no rules at all. Fighting, shooting, etc., was a life of excitement that was heading nowhere, when you are out there you don't have a level head. As much as I loved all of those things and the attention it would bring, deep in my heart, I wanted to be liked and when you are out there doing whatever, whenever to whomever, you must know that somehow, someway the law of reciprocity will kick in! That's right, it's coming back, but often you don't see the prepared harvest of all of the bad seeds you've sown until you are ready to change your life for the better. It is in those times you start to think, when you can't get that good job or rent that nice place because of a criminal record, so much of what I was going through was heavy.

In those dark moments, I had to continue to see myself beyond my condition and know in my knower that God would take all my mess and give me a message.

Right in this moment, I was about to go in another direction, but I sincerely felt led to stay on the path I'm on to really deal with my challenges, mindsets and perhaps some fears of how things would turn out. I remember the shame I brought to my family, the hurt I brought to my parents and I had to live with that. I was determined to show them that I was a better person and that I was going to overcome the obstacles that I faced, which I created myself. It was time to pull it together and become who I was meant to be, but it wouldn't be easy. I knew I had to focus and develop a different strategy. The fear of failure would often grip me, however I had this awesome feeling or should I say anticipation that I would overcome and that I would ultimately be successful. I remember thinking "I'm supposed to be successful". I had felt that way for years. See all of us have a dream or a vision and it's like the preview to your destiny. Just like movie previews are designed to get you to attend a movie, so are our dreams and visions. They're designed to get us to our destiny! I had dreams and I understood that God had a plan for my life, but that doesn't make things any easier. You must be prepared to take it to the extreme if you are going to fulfill destiny. I had to endure more, try harder and believe for greater if I was going to become who I was destined to be.

So in the process of becoming I had a lot of issues floating across my mind because I knew I had made enough bad decisions to last a lifetime and I knew there were people who wouldn't readily accept the fact that I was on a different path!

Thoughts of failure would cross my mind, however I knew that it wouldn't be a perfect transition, but it would be a worthy transition because the only way to live without error is to never attempt to accomplish anything.

So I was in for the long hall. I wasn't going to allow past failures to dictate my future. I believed, prepared and hoped for something big to happen. In the bible, peter is on the boat fishing and he fished all night but caught nothing! Then Jesus shows up and tells him to launch out into the deep and to let down his nets for a draught. Peter had to overcome the fact that he had been fishing all night and caught nothing. In essence, in order for us to move forward and advance in life this phrase "launch out into the deep" simply means to intensify your efforts. It means to go harder and often, in order for us to do that, we must overcome our last failure and start looking ahead because, most times, our latest failure is our greatest challenge. So in the midst of my transition, I had to learn how to put certain things behind me and how to focus on the hope of future events.

THE REVELATION

It's time to get linked up with purpose and destiny because there is an unstoppable shift.

-From Sermon I Preached

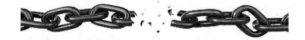

n this chapter titled The Revelation, I will reveal some of he thoughts that I had to develop while I was ransitioning. It's not easy to re-invent yourself and often people that knew you before, your reinvention, are not hat willing to let go of your past. Therefore, you must levelop tough skin and give people the benefit of the loubt and allow their challenges of you to become estimonies of strength and fortitude. After all, you can't ifford to crumble in the face of criticism. If so, then you von't be able to move to the next level of your life. So of course I'm a preacher and people didn't want to accept hat. They didn't want to give me a chance and I had to give them the benefit of doubt and at the same time, not allow their opinions to dictate my destiny. What I mean is this. I'm giving them the benefit of the doubt. I had a bad reputation and I had to own up to the fact that their view of me was one I created. As I tell men whenever I'm privileged to offer advice, "you must be willing to prove yourself" because the world is not indebted to you. However, the contrary is more of a reality. As I stated I was giving the benefit of the doubt, but not allowing opinions to dictate my destiny. I came to the conclusion that, "you must know who you are so the criticism of others will strengthen your cause". You must learn to use doubt, naysayers and criticisms as building blocks to your destiny. To recreate yourself, that's really what you are doing. You are recreating your image, building your worth and working towards a greater outcome. However it is more than a notion. It's easier said than done because of all of the negative emotions and feelings that I had it became a day to day struggle trying to be a better person and walk in your God ordained office and to make sure that you don't choke in the process. I felt the pressure of my surroundings. On one hand, I had a very small group that was cheering for me. Then I had the other group just waiting to see if my change was real and in their hearts hoping I would fail. I must admit that I believe my greatest challenge was internal. I believe it was my negative view of myself that I had from a child I never really did anything that made anyone truly proud of me. I was on a mission that was filled with hope and hopelessness. I mean I struggled and I had faith and I believed. Then I doubted and was filled with fear because feelings of guilt would come. I had sold crack to a man with a family and it was his rent money he used to buy it. I would ride by and see his children and would totally be unconcerned about the situation. I sold to a woman who has no man and has children and the crack is taking pamper and food money from them. You knew she was selling her body if she wanted to get high and keep her money. I had a lot of thoughts about who I was or should I say who I used to be. There was this feeling of wanting to totally redeem myself and the passion to do so was equally matched with the feeling of inadequacy. I had to eventually come to grips with the fact that I was from a decent family who was deeply rooted in the church and that I was raised to have certain principles in place, even though those principles were not played out in front of me as much as they were imparted to me. I had to determine that if I was going to turn it around, in spite of those who would rather see me fail, in spite of the feelings of being an underachiever. I had to draw the conclusion that my time is now! I had to say its time to move forward and that greatness was calling me and that there was a platform carved out for me to stand tall! All I had to do was start moving forward.

Moving forward is more than a notion, but it is possible. I believe the problem most people have in moving forward is that they believe that everything in their past has to be somehow over. They must have healed from every scar and every bad situation in order to move forward. Not so! Sometimes we must move forward while wounds are still fresh. This is war, that's right, it's an all-out War out here to succeed in life and accomplish your dreams and aspirations. In real combat, when a soldier is injured his comrades will do whatever it takes to help him to move forward and get out of the line of fire. This is not the time to pamper the wound. Sometimes, while they are in agony and pain, they have to keep moving because it's a matter of life or death. That's how we must look at destiny, as if it's a matter of life and death. If I don't keep it moving, I could lose my opportunity at life. I had so many mixed feelings because I knew I had to better myself and I had this great feeling of what if. You know that little cloud of doubt that's often tucked away in our hearts, that when we roar like a lion it meows like a little kitten. You know the one, when you barking like a rock wilder and its barking like a poodle. The struggle was for me to ultimately move forward with all of my baggage, my doubts and fears. I had to just move forward. Moving forward, you must understand that you cannot allow the fact that you may have issues, scars and wounds from your past to stop you. I had to figure out how to not allow it to affect me and hinder my progress. The apostle Paul, from the bible, who had to overcome his past in order to grip his destiny, said we must "forget those things which are behind and press towards the mark" Philippians 3:14. That term "press" suggests to us that there is blockage it assures us that there would be obstacles that had to be overcome; there would be restrictions that would have to be broken. We must note that it's easy to walk in fear and doubt when you look at the mountains of success and wonder. All of us have that fight in us; we just need to learn how to tap into it. Eventually, I had to shift my mind to think like I was in a war. Most, or should I say all, battles are fought on the landscape of our minds because our minds are so complex. In our mind, we can think positive and then with that same mind, turn around and think negative. In our minds, we can store information and with that same mind we forget. In our minds, we can find hope and then with that same mind, we can turn around and doubt and fear. I had to begin to believe that anything is possible. I had to believe that a boy that was born in the hood and lived in poverty and didn't have much growing up, could become something much more and could break the curse of his past decisions. I believed that same boy could step into a new season of life. I had to believe in myself and who God had called me to be. I needed to believe that all of my issues, my negative views of myself, and the negative views that others had about me couldn't stop me.

Against all odds, I had to maintain high levels of enthusiasm and excitement about my change for the better and all of the opportunities that would come with it. When transitioning your life, you must believe that it's your God given right to live life in a positive fashion. You must believe that for some reason, beyond all of the things you've done wrong in life, that if still here, it didn't kill you then it made you better.

A revelation is the unveiling of a truth that guides you to a greater reality. It's the "aha" moments we have when we suddenly get it and began to realize that we can become better, that we can accomplish any goal that the past has established in life. It must be used as fuel to the fire. It must ignite your passion to pursue better and believe that you've already made bad choices and you've already paid the price. The new you is excited about the new opportunities and possibilities that are laid before you. Your time is now! Your decisions now will reflect the new path and direction you're headed and the only people you surround yourself with will be people of substance and purpose. I had to believe that I could handle anything and that I could fit into the mold of success and be around those that were successful. I must admit, if I haven't said it before now, I never wanted to be a preacher/pastor, however I fully believe it was the path that was divinely selected for me. Trust me; I'm not saying that in order for your life to turn around you must become a preacher. Although I don't necessarily believe that you just become a preacher. I believe if you are a preacher then life will somehow lead you in the direction where you will began to get the "revelation" of what you should be. Just like if you are an athlete, or an actor, journalist etc…, whatever you are designed to be ultimately it will be revealed and the path will manifest.

THE AFTERMATH

(THE RESULTS)

My destiny has been preordained, prearranged and set in place by God and it's time to get it.

-From Sermon I Preached

The aftermath is such an appropriate name for this chapter. I revealed the results of my decisions and also shared with you where I am now. What can I say, it's the last chapter, the aftermath or the conclusion to a story that is not the truest conclusion because my journey continues. Needless to say I've been through a lot in my life. I've had to struggle often in life from a child until I became a grown man, but through it all my testimony is that I'm here. Here is where you may ask. I'm a pastor now. Yes a pastor, and not only am I pastoring but this is my second pastorate. The first church I pastored was in rural area Arkansas and it was an incredible church with incredible people. I was about 31 and I was excited because this was finally what I considered as the stamp of approval on my life. I'm the spiritual leader of others. People had finally begun to see me as a new man. After all, they voted me in and it kind of went like this. A friend told me of a church that needed a pastor and he thought I would be a good fit because they didn't want a pastor who was single. I was a few years into my marriage to an incredible woman and we were excited about being in ministry and actually taking ministry to the next level by pastoring a church. Now I must insert this, I spoke earlier that if you wanted to shift your life from its tough past then you must surround yourself with the right people. I must admit that my wife was and is still a very goal oriented woman who is very much an inspiration in my life. As a matter of fact, when I met her I was a grown man in ministry with no education and the sad part is I actually made it to the 12th grade. I missed too many days and then had an altercation in the office when they said my credits weren't enough to graduate. That didn't go well at all. I meet this beautiful woman and I was working a decent job and I was in the ministry, but had not received my high school diploma. This woman believed in me so much that she encouraged me to get my GED and go to college and I did. She drove to Arkansas to pick me up and take me to school to finish my GED pretest so I could get into school. I can't explain how excited I was about having a woman in my life that pushed me and truly believed in me, but there is much more to be said about my wife and children that I may share in another book.

I heard of a church through a friend and he wanted me to go by their bible study. I did after driving and driving and driving deep into the country. I was nervous, but confident. I went in and I listened as the deacon gave his best attempt to teach. They waited until the end and they asked me to make comments on the subject matter they were discussing. I did what I do best; I opened my mouth and allowed my knowledge and insight into biblical matters to flow. This brings me to another very important point, when opportunity presents itself and it's your time to shine and shift the direction of your life you must be ready. You can make excuses or you can make history. That's what I did. So they asked me to come back the next week and teach the whole class and I did. They then asked if I could come and preach in a couple of weeks. I was told that after I preached the first time that they called a meeting after church and many decided that I was their pastor. They invited me back a second time and now it was time to wait and see what the outcome would be. What's incredible about this is that they were already deep in the process of finding new leadership. They were literally at the end of the process and no more preachers were to be submitted to the congregation and then I came along. So there I was, in the running to become the pastor of what was considered to be one of the more prominent churches and oldest, historical churches in the area. Even though it was not a large church, it had influence and I knew some people knew my past. Not only that, pastors didn't think that I would be selected to lead because I was young and inexperienced and that they would go with a more experienced leader. I remember waiting and receiving a phone call from the chairman of the deacon board. He called me during the process to inform me that I was the favored candidate for the position and to keep quiet about it because he was breaking the rules by informing me too soon. Now that's powerful because I was a person who had spent much of his life breaking rules and now, on the positive side, someone is breaking rules for me. Let me say this because anytime someone breaks the rules for you it is called favor, it's God intervening on your behalf to bring a desired outcome!

Finally, they called and said "hey pastor" you are now our new pastor and we want you to start in a few weeks. This is it! I've arrived and I was accepted. I'm a part of another world because I'm in ministry. I felt such excitement and felt so grateful that after all I had put my parents through that something good was happening. It wasn't me calling saying hey I'm in jail can you come get me out. This time, I was calling my mother to tell her that I was the new pastor of Mt. Pisgah Missionary Baptist church! I was being elevated in life and it felt great. A few weeks passed and I got up for my first Sunday as their pastor. I was nervous, but excited and ready to go. The night before, my mother called and said I was going to church with you in the morning, so come and get me. I was like wow! She was attending her brother's church that she loved dearly, but now her first born is a pastor and she was coming with me. What a time we had on that Sunday. We laughed, we cried and rejoiced. After church, I dropped my mother off and my wife and I continued the celebration. We could hardly sleep for talking about church. Here is where things got a little gloomy. The next day, my mother called and said I need you to bring me some needles so I can take my shots. She was a diabetic. After my meeting, I went to get the needles and drop them off. I stayed in the living room while my wife went to the back to take my mother her needles and she talked with her for a minute. They laughed then my wife came from the back smiling and I yelled "see ya later ma." I went home and around 9 or 10 the next morning the phone rang. It was my dad and he was crying. He said, "Kevin, you need to get here now your mom will not wake up, she is dead!" I said I was on my way, as if I could change the situation. I hung up the phone, yelled, and then called my wife almost out of my mind. I told her the situation and that I couldn't drive to get her. She came home. I was literally walking in the middle of the street because I was feeling as if I was losing my mind. I was spaced out and didn't know what to do. I said to myself, "God this ain't right, the moment I get my life together and things are turning around for me, you allow this." I remembered a conversation that my mother and I had not long before I became a pastor and she said, "I asked God to allow me to live long enough to see my children become grown and take care of themselves." It's almost as if she willed herself to live and after she saw me as a pastor she was at peace and could end her suffering. I was an emotional wreck and felt so alone in the world after her death. I remember the deacons calling saying to me I could take some time off and allow myself to heal. This was by far the most trying time in my life and I felt as if I finally lost and I felt my world was in such confusion. On one hand I was blessed because I was a new, young pastor with a great church. Then, on the other hand, I had lost one of the most important people in my life. If anything could break me, certainly this would. I began to reminisce about my mother and how proud of me she was. She would light up when I would preach, giving her stamp of approval with every smile or nod of the head or lifting of the hands. Somehow, I found strength and I knew she would've wanted me to press on. One thing I often tell people is that we do what we do not just for ourselves but for those that love us.

So I jumped into my new position full speed ahead. I was like wow! I felt so accomplished; my church had musicians and a new church van and money in the bank, so we were ready! Only one problem, my past is still lingering around because I was still on probation for a drug charge years prior. Now I was a pastor. It was a very perplexing feeling for me to be a spiritual leader and somewhat of a problem solver for others, yet have this major issue of my own that will not go away. When the time approached for me to go and see my probation officer, it was depressing. I literally felt something come over me, In the beginning of my probation, it was scary because I was in Arkansas and I can remember living in fear that I would run into or that one of my parishioners would see me go into the probation office, or that my probation officer would have to come by the church to verify my employment or speak to a deacon or secretary, since I didn't have a check stub. It was hard and I always wondered if I had just sat down and talked with the probation officers and explained would they understand how the church worked, even though they knew somewhat of my past because I would often mention it during my sermons, I never said I was still paying for my wrongs.

So I'm married and I have moved to Tennessee. I had my probation transferred and I was thinking I could pastor in Arkansas and I live in Tennessee, so the chances of my church members seeing me was slim. Now I had new problems, because these officers were mean and it appeared as if every time I got used to an officer they would give me another who was meaner than the one before.

By this time I was getting invites to other churches, even in Memphis. What I feared the most just had to happen. I was walking in to see my officer and I heard someone say "Hey Pastor Whitaker." The feeling I had at that moment, my heart fell into my socks and I was paralyzed but I turned and said hey and when they came in I could remember the church member just watching to see why was I there. Now as I said these Tennessee officers were tough, and they didn't take me serious as a pastor. I was just another client or criminal to them. For me, this was painful because I am a pastor being treated like a convict. It appeared to me that I was still trapped by my past, as if nothing in my life had changed for the better. I recall writing to the Tennessee Board of Probation saying that I was a pastor and I have been in ministry for some years now and how I didn't deserve to be treated like that!

And of course there was no response. I had to remember was guilty of a crime and this was my punishment. Please understand the feelings I had as my new position in life was being threatened and haunted by my old position in life. I was determined not to allow bad decisions of the past to dictate and control my future. I had to realize that this wouldn't last always. One of the greatest challenges in life is waiting. You have to wait on things to turn around, wait on your time. What really helped me through these trying moments in life was the fact I had been through and survived so much up to this point and there had to be a moment when my season would come because that's the reality, just as in the natural seasons come and go, You can't pray for winter to come in the summer or spring to come in the fall because things are divinely orchestrated to be a certain way. In life there are seasons and no matter what they will change! That's the inevitable truth. I had that in mind and till this day whenever I'm faced with a great challenge I think about seasons and how they must change.

Back to the story, I had an incredible church and I had a great vision and I felt as if they wouldn't or couldn't support what I wanted to do, so I began to pray and while praying a friend who is now my brother Apostle Lee Harris Jr. told me I shouldn't be restricted as a Pastor. He told me that I should start my own church so I could have more creative control and more power to make decisions I thought would be beneficial for the ministry.

That sounded good but I was comfortable, even though my vision was being frustrated. One day, there was a group of preachers and we were going into the Fed Ex Forum to watch the Grizzlies play the Lakers and my now dear friend and Brother Bishop Donald Hawkins who I had just met turned to me and said, "The church you are at now is not where you will be." Needless to say I was kind of thinking I don't know you, but when God wants to bring clarity to your life, he will use whoever he chooses.

So soon after this episode, I traveled to St. Louis with some other friends to Bishop Hawkins church. The preacher who was scheduled to preach got up, after being introduced, turned around and told me God is moving you from where you are now! WOW, I was amazed because I have been told three times which confirmed what I was feeling! It was time to resign from my already existing church and start to walk towards my destiny. You must understand that comfort and fear is the enemy of progress and if you are going to get the optimal results from your life choices, you cannot be afraid, or as Joyce Meyer, world renown evangelist, once said, "Even if you are afraid MOVE FORWARD."

So guess what, I resigned and started fresh with no money and no members. It's a different world starting a church unless you already have followers and I didn't so now I was announcing it on my radio broadcast that I started at my former church, and I set up the official launch dates at a hotel. I invited friends and family to come to the evening service and I would launch my ministry. Now as I began to dive into the world of church planting I soon learned that if you weren't clicked up with the good ole boy system it would make things kind of difficult. However, perseverance is always critical when you are moving into unchartered waters. My life had been through many challenges including divorce but God sent a woman in my life specifically designed to help the vision of my life

So then as my ministry began to take off, I was newly married to the woman of my dreams and I was very reluctant to share my past with her. However, I shared a little at a time, so that she wouldn't be too concerned about the man she was getting involved with. She took it all in stride realizing I was so far removed from the man I used to be, at least she thought until one day my daughter called me from their mother's house and said that her mom's boyfriend was jumping on her older sister (my step daughter) and that he was threatening her and her sister. I completely lost it! Yelling and screaming, I then began to issue threats to the boyfriend letting him know I was on the way to pick up my daughters and that they should call the police because if I make it there before them it would be an ugly scene. This scared my wife she had never seen me this way. I was embarrassed because the old me had arisen! I was glad that things turned out well that day and truthfully I was only a concerned father willing to do whatever to protect his children. It appeared that my past was always lurking in the shadows, waiting on an opportunity to rise and put me in a situation that would put me in a bad place. Once, at the movie theater, I got into an altercation with two thugs for kicking my then fiancé's seat at the movie theater. Another time, after some girls in the community jumped my daughter, I went over to their house and I basically knocked and walked in at the same time and I informed them that if this happened again I would come and see them. If that wasn't enough, one day there was a knock on the door. It was an investigator. I said yes and she said, "I need to talk with you." It was about being a character witness for a friend of mines who at the time was on death row and they were desperately trying to get him off. So my past was always an issue, even though these things happened early in my ministry. It was still a thorn in my flesh. It was as if I couldn't escape my past, but I simply just had to realize that time would eventually be my friend and consistency in ministry would be the proof that I was a man on a different path.

These things that I dealt with were just a harsh reality of a life without discipline. Then one day my past became all too real as I received a letter in the mail saying that if I didn't come up with about $7000 dollars, I would go to prison. This was an old fine from an even older drug charge. I was paying on a fine for about ten years to the sheriff dept. and I would always get a receipt however over the years I had moved a couple of times and lost my receipts. I had no proof of paying and they were only giving me a few days to come up with the money. It was crucial, I was furious because I knew that someone in the office was pocketing my fine money!

When God has a plan for your life it often appears to be an inevitable truth that will come to past, so I was faced with at least 6 months not in the county jail but the big house, The State Penitentiary. I was not certain of where I would get the money, so I started to make plans to shut down my church and do my time in jail, but my wife said no. She was determined to get the money. She was asking family, but no one could or would help and time was winding down and as a last resort, my wife called a local Pastor and his wife. He pastored a mega church in the city and they decided it was certain through prayer and discernment, that they would pay it for me, which to me was confirmation of my destiny. A stranger would actually pay this money for me and allow me to continue my ministry. Not only did the fact that the pastor and his wife paid the money amaze and humble me, but also that my wife believed in me enough to go out on a limb, swallow her pride, put her reputation on the line and ask total strangers for almost $7000. This also proves my point that if you are going to make it in life and press on past all of the potential disasters that life can bring, you must have people in your life that believe in you and what you are called to do. Regardless of the challenges that your past may bring, you honor their support by actually being who you claim to be. Often this requires what I like to call going hard! That means you continue o overcome and overthrow any and everything that attempts to continually hold you back. It's that moment when destiny overrides fear, error, and disappointment. Going hard means you may have excuses, but you're not going to take the liberty to use them. You're going to press past the place of excuses and activate your faith and continue to believe, even when the test you face are unbelievable. I say this all the time, everywhere I go. You must refuse to be stopped. It's a faith that declares if I can't run past it, I will run through it and if I can't run through it I will go over it and if they won't let me over it, I will go under, in other words whatever it takes to win in life that is within the boundaries of doing what's right you do it! And if you are restricted by your past that just means you must plan more and work harder. A piece of grass will grow from under the concrete, because it refuses to stay under! That has to be your mindset! This is my story and at this point in my ministry, I have traveled many places to preach. I have been a guest on TBN, Word Network, TV 57, and I've also hosted my own radio and television broadcast titled the "Raising the Standard" show. I've been a guest on various radio shows and graced the cover of magazine "Majesty Now" and I was featured in Fresh Oil magazine as well, which afforded me the opportunity to share the wisdom obtained from a life that has been down a path of destruction only to find destiny, I say to you, YOU TO ARE TOO HARD TO BREAK! GO HARDER!

APOSTLE
KEVINWHITAKER

BIOGRAPHY

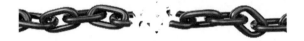

Apostle Kevin Whitaker is the Senior Pastor of Epic Church, Intl located in Memphis, TN. Apostle was reared in rural and urban Arkansas where he had to overcome less than favorable circumstances and made a host of bad decisions which all play a part in his passion to see people delivered.

He has hosted his own radio show and had his own telecast on Good News TV. Apostle Whitaker has been seen on the Memphis branch of TBN, TV 57 in Atlanta. He has also been a guest on the Vernell Galbreath show on the Word Network.

Apostle Whitaker has been instrumental in partnering with the Girls and Boys Club in the local area, meeting with the head of the Gang Unit, District Attorney and former gang leaders. He is currently working in the school system dealing with troubled youth providing guidance and motivation to finish their education and attend college.

Traveling the country to preach the Gospel and the Apostolic Mantle on his life invigorates those around him to be the best they can be. He serves as mentor and Spiritual Father to other Pastors and is considered by many as a true servant leader. Apostle Whitaker flows in the prophetic and deliverance and is known to shift atmospheres.

CONTACT INFORMATION

Mailing Address:
P.O. Box 280507
Memphis TN, 38168

Facebook: Apostle Kevin Whitaker
Twitter: @apreacha
Website: APOSTLEKWHITAKER.ORG

CPSIA information can be obtained
at www.ICGtesting.com
Printed in the USA
LVOW10s2108120517

534338LV00009B/18/P